Thomas Edison:

Quotes & Facts

By Blago Kirov

First Edition

I0412992

*****

Thomas Edison: Quotes & Facts
*****

Foreword

Everyone steals in commerce and industry. I've stolen a lot, myself. But I know how to steal! They don't know how to steal!

This book is an anthology of 92 quotes from Thomas Edison and 70 selected facts about Thomas Edison.

I start where the last man left off.

Everyone steals in commerce and industry. I've stolen a lot, myself. But I know how to steal! They don't know how to steal!

All bibles are man-made.

Great ideas originate in the muscles.

I am proud of the fact that I never invented weapons to kill.

Show me a thoroughly satisfied man and I will show you a failure.

Anything that won't sell, I don't want to invent. Its sale is proof of utility, and utility is success.

Be courageous. I have seen many depressions in business. Always America has emerged from these stronger and more prosperous. Be brave as your fathers before you. Have faith! Go forward!

Being busy does not always mean real work. The object of all work is production or accomplishment and to either of these ends there must be forethought, system, planning, intelligence, and honest purpose, as well as perspiration. Seeming to do is not doing

Discontent is the first necessity of progress.

Thomas Edison was home-schooled.

The Edison's kinetoscope was a machine where you put in a coin, look through a peephole in a cabinet, and watch a short motion picture.

When Thomas Edison lay dying at his home in New Jersey, newspaper reporters were anxiously awaiting a sign from his wife of his death. She signaled Edison's passing by turning a light on, not off, in his bedroom. Thomas Edison reportedly drank "wine coca" - a medicinal tonic made from coca leaves, the same type of coca that cocaine is extracted from - during marathon research sessions that ran into the night.

Using a primitive cylinder and foil device, Thomas Edison created the first known recording of a human voice: his own, reciting the poem "Mary Had A Little Lamb".

Thomas Edison was close friend of Henry Ford.

In 1931, when Thomas Edison died, his estate was estimated at well over $12 million. His estate included shares of Thomas A. Edison, Inc. valued at more than $10 million, $1,342,000 in United States bonds, $48,000 in railroad bonds, $48,000 in cash, and 76,000 shares in 37 different companies that no longer exist.

Nikola Tesla briefly worked for Edison as a technician but quit after arguing with Thomas Edison one too many times.

Thomas Edison built his own science laboratory at the age of 10. This was built in the basement of his home.

Some Facts about Thomas Edison

Thomas Edison was home-schooled.

The Edison's kinetoscope was a machine where you put in a coin, look through a peephole in a cabinet, and watch a short motion picture.

When Thomas Edison lay dying at his home in New Jersey, newspaper reporters were anxiously awaiting a sign from his wife of his death. She signaled Edison's passing by turning a light on, not off, in his bedroom.

Thomas Edison reportedly drank "wine coca" - a medicinal tonic made from coca leaves, the same type of coca that cocaine is extracted from - during marathon research sessions that ran into the night.

Using a primitive cylinder and foil device, Thomas Edison created the first known recording of a human voice: his own, reciting the poem "Mary Had A Little Lamb".
Thomas Edison was close friend of Henry Ford.

In 1931, when Thomas Edison died, his estate was estimated at well over $12 million. His estate included shares of Thomas A. Edison, Inc. valued at more than $10 million, $1,342,000 in United States bonds, $48,000 in railroad bonds, $48,000 in cash, and 76,000 shares in 37 different companies that no longer exist.

Nikola Tesla briefly worked for Edison as a technician but quit after arguing with Thomas Edison one too many times.

Thomas Edison built his own science laboratory at the age of 10. This was built in the basement of his home.

Thomas Alva Edison was born on the 11th of February, 1847 in Milan, Ohio.

Thomas Edison was preceded in birth by his six siblings, Marion, William, Callie, Harriet, Samuel and Eliza. His family was not poor, as the myths would have it, but at the same time they were not so wealth.

Thomas Edison was inducted into the National Inventors Hall of Fame, 1973.

Thomas Edison's first inventions include an electric vote recorder and a stock ticker.

Thomas Edison made several experimental short films, some lasting only several seconds, mostly to test his equipment. One film, which features a man sneezing, runs for one and one-half seconds.

His son, Charles Edison, was a secretary of the U.S. Navy and Governor of New Jersey.

Though his hearing was impaired from the age of 12, Thomas Edison said that it did not bother him because it helped him concentrate better.

Thomas Edison becomes a telegraph operator at age of 15, because he saved a telegraph operator's son from the path of a railroad car. As a reward, the operator gave him free telegraph lessons - which started Edison on his way of becoming one of the greatest men in history.

Edison's light bulbs were financed by Morgan and Vanderbilt.

Mina Miller bore Thomas Edison three children, Madeleine, Charles and Theodore Miller.

Mina Miller outlived Thomas Edison by 16 years.

From 1862 to 1868 Edison worked in the telegraphy industry, where he learned much about mechanical devices. During this time, he also came into contact with a number of important individuals, including the current king of inventors, Alexander Graham Bell.

Thomas Edison did not begin speaking until he was four years old, prompting some adults around him to speculate that he might be retarded. Thomas was not retarded, but he may have suffered from what we now term 'Attention Deficit Disorder' (ADD) and dyslexia.

Thomas Edison invented the first incandescent light bulb in 1879.

Thomas Edison holds around 1,093 U.S. patents as well as many other patents in the United Kingdom, Germany and France.

Thomas Edison enjoyed communication with Morse code so much, that he proposed marriage to his girlfriend in it, and nicknamed his children "Dot" and "Dash".

In 1876, Thomas Edison, with the support of several financiers, including J. P. Morgan, set up a laboratory for inventing purposes in small New Jersey town Menlo Park.

Thomas Edison married his first wife Mary Stilwell at the age of 24. She was his employee. They had 3 children together.

After his first wife Mary died, Thomas Edison married Mina Miller.

In his later years, Thomas Edison often committed social faux pas by making racist and anti-Semitic comments before the press.

At the age of 14 Thomas Edison saved a 3 year old boy - Jimmie MacKenzie from being hit by a train at the Grand Trunk Railroad.

Thomas Edison had very humble beginnings. He even sold newspapers on trains and vegetables to be able to add to his income.

While Edison's partial deafness was the subject a great deal of speculation and mythology, it is generally assumed that it was caused by a childhood bout of scarlet fever.

Thomas Edison is venerated by a sect of the Shinto faith as "the god of electricity".

Many of Edison's experimental films were made in a small wooden building dubbed "The Black Maria" because it resembled a police wagon of the same name. Edison's Black Maria was built on a lot next to his lab and office. The building, essentially a large wooden shed covered with tar paper, was small enough that it was mounted on circular tracks so it could be turned to accommodate sunlight through an opening in the roof. The original has long since burned down, but a reproduction of the structure is located at the Edison National Historic Site in West Orange, New Jersey.

Thomas Edison is credited with the invention of sprocket cinema film.

Edison's electrographic vote-recorder (U.S. patent no. 90,646) was capable of recording a yes or no vote, and while it worked, it was not well-received by Washington politicians.

Other inventions to Edison's credit include cellophane tape, waxed paper, an improved version of the typewriter keyboard, and "the electric pencil", a forerunner to today's fax machine.

Thomas Edison rarely if ever slept a normal 8 hour period. He preferred to take "siestas" throughout the day, and kept cots in his office and lab.

While Thomas Edison is often erroneously credited with the invention of the incandescent light bulb, he only perfected it. Similar bulbs were already in existence, but they were expensive, did not last long, and gave off a bad smell. By developing a low-cost, long-lasting, carbonized cotton filament, he made electrical light cheap enough to be financially practical.

Thomas Edison is pictured on a 3¢ US postage stamp in the Famous Americans and Inventors series, issued 11 February 1947 - centennial year of his birth.

The last years of Edison's life were plagued by financial failures, including plans to make houses out of poured formed concrete and making rubber from goldenrod.

Thomas Edison is depicted on the obverse of a USA $1 commemorative silver coin celebrating the 125th anniversary of the light bulb.

Thomas Edison was awarded a Congressional Gold Medal, 29 May 1928.

After the invention of the phonograph in 1877, Thomas Edison was thereafter known as 'The Wizard of Menlo Park' in New Jersey.

Thomas Edison played virtually no role in the production of individual films by the movie company that bore his name.

The period from 1879 to 1900 is called the Age of Edison. This span of time is the period when Thomas Edison produced and perfected most of his devices.

Thomas Edison often wore dirty shirts and shabby working clothes. Nevertheless, his associates describe him a humorous type of person and had a genuine affection for his family.

Thomas Edison is father of Charles Edison.

Edison's company was considerably late to become involved in the recorded music business.

While Thomas Edison did invent the phonograph, his intention was to market it as a business dictation machine.

The concept of recorded music never crossed Edison's mind.

Edison's son supposedly captured his last breath in a glass jar. The jar is on display at the reconstructed Menlo Park at Greenfield Village in Dearborn, Michigan.

Despite his company producing one of the earliest advertisements for cigarettes (Admiral Cigarettes), Thomas Edison became an ardent anti-smoking advocate; going so far as to say that he would not hire anyone who smoked.

Thomas Edison invented the cylinder recorder (phonograph) but it was Emile Berliner who created the flat disc, Edison licensed the patent from him.

Thomas Edison invented the Kinetograph camera and the peephole kinetoscope viewer.

The Edison Manufacturing Company's earliest films were produced solely to demonstrate the use of the peephole viewer.

His father, Samuel Edison, was of Dutch ancestry and his mother, Nancy Elliot, was of English decent.

Thomas Edison was member of the Academy of Motion Picture Arts & Sciences - AMPAS.

Thomas Edison invented also an improved electrical storage battery where he had spent eight years and a million dollars. This battery was widely used in electric cars and even to power submarines.

Edison's attempts to force independent filmmakers to use his patented movie equipment resulted in an exodus of the film industry out West to a little town called Hollywood-land, now known as Hollywood.

The first commercial power system was developed by Thomas Edison in 1882, when he began lighting homes in New York. His company began producing electricity for New York City homes in 1882 using direct current.

By 1876, Thomas Edison had amassed $40,000 through the sale of various telegraphic devices.

In 1889, Italy made Thomas Edison a Grand Officer of the Crown.

Edison's very first copyrighted film was a recording of a sneeze. 'The Great Train Robbery' was created in 1903, produced by Edison and directed by Edwin S. Porter. The short film, based on an actual train robbery pulled off by Butch Cassidy and his gang, became the inspiration for an entire industry, though Edison himself never had much financial success from it

His discovery and documentation of the Edison Effect eventually helped lead to the development of the vacuum tube, a key component for early radios, televisions and computers.

Thomas Edison received awards from the governments of Chile, Britain, Japan, Russia, and many other nations.

In association with 2 business partners, Thomas Edison invented a new type of printing telegraph called a 'gold printer' that he sold to Western Union for $15,000.

Edison's second patent, an improved stock indicator machine, was sold to Western Union for $40,000.

In 1878, Edison began important research on electric lighting. He saw a demonstration of a carbon arc light that was really bright. So, Edison started to work an incandescent light, which would be less bright, for everyday use. In 1879, Edison tested a carbon filament made from burned sewing thread and it worked.

Thomas Edison was involved in the incorporation of G.E. General Electric Company in 1892. It would soon go toe-to-toe with its major early rival, Westinghouse, who employed Nikola Tesla, the developer of alternating current.

His Words

I start where the last man left off.

Everyone steals in commerce and industry. I've stolen a lot, myself. But I know how to steal! They don't know how to steal!

All bibles are man-made.

Great ideas originate in the muscles.

I am proud of the fact that I never invented weapons to kill.

Show me a thoroughly satisfied man and I will show you a failure.

Anything that won't sell, I don't want to invent. Its sale is proof of utility, and utility is success.

Be courageous. I have seen many depressions in business. Always America has emerged from these stronger and more prosperous. Be brave as your fathers before you. Have faith! Go forward!

Being busy does not always mean real work. The object of all work is production or accomplishment and to either of these ends there must be forethought, system, planning, intelligence, and honest purpose, as well as perspiration. Seeming to do is not doing

Discontent is the first necessity of progress.

During all those years of experimentation and research, I never once made a discovery. All my work was deductive, and the results I achieved were those of invention, pure and simple. I would construct a theory and work on its lines until I found it was untenable. Then it would be discarded at once and another theory evolved. This was the only possible way for me to work out the problem. ... I speak without exaggeration when I say that I have constructed 3,000 different theories in connection with the electric light, each one of them reasonable and apparently likely to be true. Yet only in two cases did my experiments prove the truth of my theory. My chief difficulty was in constructing the carbon filament. . . . . Every quarter of the globe was ransacked by my agents, and all sorts of the queerest materials used, until finally the shred of bamboo, now utilized by us, was settled upon.

Everything comes to him who hustles while he waits.

Failure is really a matter of conceit. People don't work hard because, in their conceit, they imagine they'll succeed without ever making an effort. Most people believe that they'll wake up some day and find themselves rich. Actually, they've got it half right, because eventually they do wake up.

Five percent of the people think; ten percent of the people think they think; and the other eighty-five percent would rather die than think.

Genius is 1 percent inspiration and 99 percent perspiration.

Hell! there ain't no rules around here! We are tryin' to accomplish somep'n!

I consider Paine our greatest political thinker. As we have not advanced, and perhaps never shall advance, beyond the Declaration and Constitution, so Paine has had no successors who extended his principles. Although the present generation knows little of Paine's writings, and although he has almost no influence upon contemporary thought, Americans of the future will justly appraise his work. I am certain of it.

I believe in the existence of a Supreme Intelligence pervading the Universe.

I do not believe in the God of the theologians; but that there is a Supreme Intelligence I do not doubt,

I find my greatest pleasure, and so my reward, in the work that precedes what the world calls success.

I find out what the world needs. Then I go ahead and try to invent it

I have always regarded Paine as one of the greatest of all Americans. Never have we had a sounder intelligence in this republic ... It was my good fortune to encounter Thomas Paine's works in my boyhood ... it was, indeed, a revelation to me to read that great thinker's views on political and theological subjects. Paine educated me, then, about many matters of which I had never before thought. I remember, very vividly, the flash of enlightenment that shone from Paine's writings, and I recall thinking, at that time, 'What a pity these works are not today the schoolbooks for all children!' My interest in Paine was not satisfied by my first reading of his works. I went back to them time and again, just as I have done since my boyhood days.

I have friends in overalls whose friendship I would not swap for the favor of the kings of the world.

I have never seen the slightest scientific proof of the religious theories of heaven and hell, of future life for individuals, or of a personal God.

I have not failed. I've just found 10,000 ways that won't work.

I know this world is ruled by infinite intelligence. Everything that surrounds us- everything that exists - proves that there are infinite laws behind it. There can be no denying this fact. It is mathematical in its precision.

I never did a day's work in my life. it was all fun.

I never did anything worth doing by accident, nor did any of my inventions come by accident; they came by work.

I never did anything worth doing by accident, nor did any of my inventions come indirectly through accident, except the phonograph. No, when I have, fully decided that a result is worth getting, I go about it, and make trial after trial, until it comes.

I owe my success to the fact that I never had a clock in my workroom. Seventy-five of us worked twenty hours every day and slept only four hours — and thrived on it.

I told [John Kruesi] I was going to record talking, and then have the machine talk back. He thought it absurd. However, it was finished, the foil was put on; I then shouted 'Mary had a little lamb', etc. I adjusted the reproducer, and the machine reproduced it perfectly.

If our nation can issue a dollar bond, it can issue a dollar bill. The element that makes the bond good, makes the bill good, also. The difference between the bond and the bill is the bond lets money brokers collect twice the amount of the bond and an additional 20%, whereas the currency pays nobody but those who contribute directly in some useful way. ... It is absurd to say our country can issue $30 million in bonds and not $30 million in currency. Both are promises to pay, but one promise fattens the usurers and the other helps the people.

If we all did the things we were capable of doing, we would literally astound ourselves.

It is astonishing what an effort it seems to be for many people to put their brains definitely and systematically to work.

Just because something doesn't do what you planned it to do doesn't mean it's useless.

Many of life's failures are people who did not realize how close they were to success when they gave up.

Many a person who could not comprehend Rousseau, and would be puzzled by Montesquieu, could understand Paine as an open book. He wrote with clarity, a sharpness of outline and exactness of speech that even a schoolboy should be able to grasp. There is nothing false, little that is subtle, and an impressive lack of the negative in Paine. He literally cried to his reader for a comprehending hour, and then filled that hour with such sagacious reasoning as we find surpassed nowhere else in American letters — seldom in any school of writing.

Maturity is often more absurd than youth and very frequently is most unjust to youth.

My mind is incapable of conceiving such a thing as a soul. I may be in error, and man may have a soul; but I simply do not believe it. What a soul may be is beyond my understanding.

Nature is truly wonderful. Only man is truly foul.

Nature is what we know. We do not know the gods of religions. And nature is not kind, or merciful, or loving. If God made me — the fabled God of the three qualities of which I spoke: mercy, kindness, love — He also made the fish I catch and eat. And where do His mercy, kindness, and love for that fish come in? No; nature made us — nature did it all — not the gods of the religions.

Nearly every person who develops an idea works at it up to the point where it looks impossible, and then gets discouraged. That's not the place to become discouraged.

Negative results are just what I want. They're just as valuable to me as positive results. I can never find the thing that does the job best until I find the ones that don't.

Non-violence leads to the highest ethics, which is the goal of all evolution. Until we stop harming all other living beings, we are still savages.

One might think that the money value of an invention constitutes its reward to the man who loves his work. But... I continue to find my greatest pleasure, and so my reward, in the work that precedes what the world calls success.

Opportunity is often missed because it comes dressed in overalls and looks like work.

Our greatest weakness lies in giving up. The most certain way to succeed; is always to try just one more time.

People who will not turn a shovel full of dirt on the project nor contribute a pound of material, will collect more money from the United States than will the People who supply all the material and do all the work. This is the terrible thing about interest ...But here is the point: If the Nation can issue a dollar bond it can issue a dollar bill. The element that makes the bond good makes the bill good also. The difference between the bond and the bill is that the bond lets the money broker collect twice the amount of the bond and an additional 20%. Whereas the currency, the honest sort provided by the Constitution pays nobody but those who contribute in some useful way. It is absurd to say our Country can issue bonds and cannot issue currency. Both are promises to pay, but one fattens the usurer and the other helps the People. If the currency issued by the People were no good, then the bonds would be no good, either. It is a terrible situation when the Government, to insure the National Wealth, must go in debt and submit to ruinous interest charges at the hands of men who control the fictitious value of gold. Interest is the invention of Satan.

Restlessness is discontent and discontent is the first necessity of progress. Show me a thoroughly satisfied man and I will show you a failure.

Results! Why, man, I have gotten a lot of results. I know several thousand things that won't work.

So far as the religion of the day is concerned, it is a damned fake ... Religion is all bunk.

The best thinking has been done in solitude. The worst has been done in turmoil.

The body is a community made up of its innumerable cells or inhabitants.

The chief function of the body is to carry the brain around.

The doctor of the future will give no medication, but will interest his patients in the care of the human frame, diet and in the cause and prevention of disease.

The doctor of the future will no longer treat the human frame with drugs, but rather will cure and prevent disease with nutrition.

The first requisite for success is the ability to apply your physical and mental energies to one problem incessantly without growing weary.

The most necessary task of civilization is to teach people how to think. It should be the primary purpose of our public schools. The mind of a child is naturally active, it develops through exercise. Give a child plenty of exercise, for body and brain. The trouble with our way of educating is that it does not give elasticity to the mind. It casts the brain into a mold. It insists that the child must accept. It does not encourage original thought or reasoning, and it lays more stress on memory than observation.

The reason a lot of people do not recognize opportunity is because it usually goes around wearing overalls looking like hard work.

The three great essentials to achieve anything worthwhile are, first, hard work; second, stick-to-itiveness; third, common sense.

The value of an idea lies in using it

There are no rules here -- we're trying to accomplish something.

There is a great directing head of people and things — a Supreme Being who looks after the destinies of the world. I am convinced that the body is made up of entities that are intelligent and are directed by this Higher Power. When one cuts his finger, I believe it is the intelligence of these entities which heals the wound. When one is sick, it is the intelligence of these entities which brings convalescence. You know that there are living cells in the body so tiny that the microscope cannot find them at all. The entities that give life and soul to the human body are finer still and lie infinitely beyond the reach of our finest scientific instruments. When these entities leave the body, the body is like a ship without a rudder — deserted, motionless and dead.

There is always a better way.

There is far more opportunity than there is ability.

There is no expedient to which a man will not go to avoid the real labor of thinking.

There is no substitute for hard work.

There is time for everything.

There will one day spring from the brain of science a machine or force so fearful in its potentialities, so absolutely terrifying, that even man, the fighter, who will dare torture and death in order to inflict torture and death, will be appalled, and so abandon war forever.

They say President Wilson has blundered. Perhaps he has, but I notice he usually blunders forward.

There's a way to do it better - find it.

This problem, once solved, will be simple.

Through all the years of experimenting and research, I never once made a discovery. I start where the last man left off. ... All my work was deductive, and the results I achieved were those of invention pure and simple.

To do much clear thinking a person must arrange for regular periods of solitude when they can concentrate and indulge the imagination without distraction.

To have a great idea, have a lot of them.

To invent, you need a good imagination and a pile of junk.

To my mind the old masters are not art; their value is in their scarcity.

Unfortunately, there seems to be far more opportunity out there than ability.... We should remember that good fortune often happens when opportunity meets with preparation.

Vision without execution is hallucination.

Waste is worse than loss. The time is coming when every person who lays claim to ability will keep the question of waste before him constantly. The scope of thrift is limitless.

We are like tenant farmers chopping down the fence around our house for fuel when we should be using Nature's inexhaustible sources of energy--sun, wind and tide. I'd put my money on the sun and solar energy. What a source of power! I hope we don't have to wait until oil and coal run out before we tackle that.

We don't know a millionth of one percent about anything.

We have but two ears and one mouth so that we may listen twice as much as we speak

We often miss opportunity because it's dressed in overalls and looks like work.

We really haven't got any great amount of data on the subject, and without data how can we reach any definite conclusions? All we have — everything — favors the idea of what religionists call the "Hereafter." Science, if it ever learns the facts, probably will find another more definitely descriptive term.

We will make electricity so cheap that only the rich will burn candles.

What a man's mind can create, man's character can control.

What you are will show in what you do.

When I have fully decided that a result is worth getting I go ahead of it and make trial after trial until it comes.

When you have exhausted all possibilities, remember this - you haven't.

Your worth consists in what you are and not in what you have.

It is very beautiful over there. (His last words)